VIRGINIA MARRIAGES
in
Rev. John Cameron's Register
and
Bath Parish Register

Published by

VIRGINIA GENEALOGICAL SOCIETY

Southern Historical Press, Inc.
Greenville, South Carolina

Please direct all correspondence and orders to:

www.southernhistoricalpress.com
or
SOUTHERN HISTORICAL PRESS, Inc.
PO BOX 1267
375 West Broad Street
Greenville, SC   29601
southernhistoricalpress@gmail.com

ISBN #0-89308-264-3

Printed in the United States of America

ABBREVIATIONS

B.   Bath Parish Register

C.   Rev. John Cameron's Register

Co.   County

M. B.   Marriage Bond

p.   Page

Res.   Residence

PREFACE

The destruction of almost all the court records of Dinwiddie and Prince George counties, Virginia, has made genealogical research in this area difficult. The assembling of these few extant marriage records by the Projects Committee of the Virginia Genealogical Society in the first of a projected series of volumes relating to the burned counties, is an event of import. The members of the Committee, Mrs. Emma R. Matheny, Chairman, Mrs. Joyce H. Lindsay, Mrs. Isobel B. Woodson, and Mrs. Helen K. Yates, are setting an example for the Society to follow.

Dinwiddie County, although formed from Prince George in 1752, has no court records prior to the fire of 1833 other than one Order Book 1789-91 and a Surveyors' Plat Book 1755-1865. The parent county of Prince George has little more preserved before 1865 - Deeds and Wills 1713-28, 1759-60, 1787-92; Inventories and accounts 1835-41; Deeds 1842-46, 1851-58; Court orders 1714-20, 1737-40, 1811-14; and Surveyors' records 1711-24, 1794-1879.

The Rev. Dr. John Cameron was rector of Bristol Parish, the eastern parish of Dinwiddie County, from 1784 until January 1794. In this period he began a register listing the marriages he performed, which he continued while rector of Nottoway Parish, Southampton County, 1794-96, and of Cumberland Parish, Lunenburg County, until his death in 1815. Earlier records of Bristol Parish were printed in The Vestry Book and Register of Bristol Parish, Virginia, 1720-1789 (Richmond, Va., 1898), transcribed by Churchill Gibson Chamberlayne.

The Register of Bath Parish, the western parish of Dinwiddie County, 1827-97, which also includes records of Saint Andrew's Parish, Brunswick County, contains marriages for the years 1826-37 and 1846-55, as well as baptisms and burials.

It is fortunate that these two manuscript volumes have been preserved. A few other Dinwiddie County marriages recorded in the Deed and Order Books have been added to help complete the record. These and some lists such as that of fourteen Dinwiddie marriages, 1818-19, published in The Virginia Magazine of History and Biography, volume 50, page 67, represent virtually all public marriage records for this area.

Also included are 161 marriage bonds of Prince George County which somehow survived the destruction of that county's records and are preserved at the Court House at Prince George.

Many will find members of their family in this volume. It is for them that the Virginia Genealogical Society was established and to help them that its efforts are directed.

John Frederick Dorman

VIRGINIA MARRIAGES

21 June 1792 - Ashly ADAMS and Mary Riddlehurst. Dinwiddie Co. C. p.14

24 Dec. 1828 - James ADAMS and Cynthia Heath. Prince George Co. M. B.

28 Nov. 1833 - Thomas ADAMS, Jr. and Elizabeth Withers at Mr.
Thomas Withers', Dinwiddie Co. B. p. 304

29 Oct. 1823 - William ADAMS and Eliza Harrison (Spinster) Prince
George Co. M. B.

14 Aug. 1850 - William A. ADAMS and Maria Ann Crump at Res. of Mr.
John Crump. C. p. 310

11 Jan. 1786 - Abram ALLEN and Mary Griffin. Prince George. C. p. 3

30 Jul. 1785 - David ALLEN and Mary Hair. Prince George. C. p. 2

22 Apr. 1786 Drury ALLEN and Salley Jeffries. Prince George. C. p. 4

14 March 1789 - Stephen ALLEY and Lucy Lee. Prince George. C. p. 10

19 Aug. 1797 - Daniel ANDERSON and Mary Read Cameron. Lunenburg. C. p. 17

26 Feb. 1786 - John ANDERSON and Betsey Norton. Dinwiddie. C. p. 3

21 Dec. 1831 - William ANDERTON and Eliza Stacy at Mr. James Stacy's,
Dinwiddie Co. B. p. 302

1 Dec. 1787 - Miles ANDREWS and Mason Perkenson. Prince George. C. p. 7

10 Nov. 1785 - Moses ANDREWS and Betsey McLeane. Dinwiddie Co. C. p. 2

21 Dec. 1825 - Thompson P. ANDREWS and Mary Eppes (Spinster) Prince
George Co. M. B.

6 July 1786 - John ANGUS and Lucy WORTHAM. Petersburg. C. p. 4

20 Sept. 1788 - Roger ATKINSON, Jr. and Agnes Poythress. Prince
George Co. C. p. 9

27 Apr. 1829 - Timothy ATKINSON and Elizabeth Glover. Prince George Co. M.B.

21 Dec. 1833 - Richard AVERY and Nanny Moore. Prince George Co. M.B.

6 May 1786 - Joseph BADGER and Nancy Shepherd. Petersburg. C. p. 4

19 Nov. 1791 - James BAIRD and Frances Cogbill. Chesterfield. C. p.13

14 Dec. 1876 - N. H. BAIRD, Jr. and Virginia E. Holcombe at Res. of N. H. Baird, Sr. in Dinwiddie. B. p. 332

2 Jan. 1806 - Irby BAKER and Dorothy Moor. Lunenburg Co. C. p. 18

1 Feb. 1848 - Rev. J. M. BANISTER (Rector of Bath Parish) and Mary Louisa Broadnax at Kingston, Dinwiddie Co., by the Rev. Edmund Withers. B. p.3

30 Mar. 1793 - John BARBER and Pricilla Evans. Chesterfield Co. C. p.1

16 Dec. 1839 - Alexander BARKER and Amijane Tatum. Prince George Co. M.

22 Dec. 1785 - Thomas BARNES and Elizabeth Anderson. Prince George Co. C.

30 June 1787 - Joseph BASS and Mary Robertson. Chesterfield Co. C. p.6

5 Nov. 1785 - John BAUGH and Anne West. Prince George Co. C. p.2

5 Feb. 1788 - Robert BAUGH and Martha Cleveland. Sussex Co. C. p.8

3 Aug. 1788 - John BAXTER and Patsey Wilkinson. Prince George Co. C. p.

1 Aug. 1792 - John BEDINGFIELD and Polly Cook. Sussex Co. C. p.14

24 Nov. 1807 - John BEGGIS and Sally M. Stokes. Lunenburg Co. C. p.19

1 June 1789 - Isham BELCHER and Winifred Royall. Chesterfield Co. C. p.

22 Dec. 1836 - Archibald BENNETT and Dorothy V. Gibbs at Mr. Tannors' B. p.305

26 Dec. 1787 - William BEST and Patsey Daniel. Prince George Co. C. p.7

4 Jan. 1815 - Charles BETTS and Martha C. Chambers. Lunenburg Co. C. p.

2 Apr. 1889 - Ernest BEVILLE and Adelia V. Perkins at Res. of B. G. Perki B. p.336

5 Nov. 1787 - Charles BINFORD and Nancy Stephens. Prince George Co. C. p

24 Sept. 1791 - William BINGHAM and Mary Grammer. Prince George Co. C. p

29 Sept. 1823 - John BIRCHETT and Elizabeth Sturdivant (Spinster). Princ George Co. M.B.

26 May 1792 - John BLACKWELL and Martha Vaughan. Prince George Co. C. p

20 June 1826 - Robert BLACKWELL and Ann Dunn. Prince George Co. M.B.

23 June 1787 - James BLAKELY and Jemima Hobbs. Petersburg. C. p.6

29 June 1808 - Edward BLAND and Rebecca Jones. Nottoway Co. C. p.19

23 Apr. 1791 - John BLAND and Mary Long. Prince George Co. C. p.12

30 Sept. 1809 - Peter BLAND and Martha W. Nash. Prince Edward Co. C. p.19

20 Nov. 1807 - Peter R. BLAND and Susanna R. Bacon. Lunenburg Co. C. p.19

11 Aug. 1829 - Richard BLAND and Martha E. Ledbetter   Prince George Co. M.B.

24 Dec. 1787 - Richard BLAND and Susanna Poythress. Prince George Co. C. p.7

12 Jan. 1790 - Bland BLANKENSHIP and Lucy Moore. Chesterfield Co. C. p.11

12 Jan. 1786 - John BLICK and Sarah Patrick. Dinwiddie Co. C. p. 3

1 Jan. 1791 - John BLICK and Rebecca White. Dinwiddie Co. C. p.12

6 Jan. 1790 - Thomas BLUNT and Judith Rives. Sussex Co. C. p.11

11 Oct. 1792 - John BOBBITT and Frances Mitchell. Sussex Co. C. p.14

15 Apr. 1829 - William H. BOISSEAU and Mary H. Thweatt at Thomas Thweatt's
Dinwiddiie Co.   B. p.301

12 Aug. 1829 - John A. BOLLING and Lucy B. Randolph at Mrs. Peggy
Randolph's, Dinwiddie Co. B. p.301

21 Feb. 1811 - Thomas BOLLING and Eliza Williams. Lunenburg Co. C. p.20

22 Dec. 1785 - John BONNER and Mary Heath Bonner. Dinwiddie Co. C. p.3

14 Nov. 1790 - Richard BOOKER and Margaret MacFarlane. Chesterfield Co.
C. p.12

19 Dec. 1788 - George BOOTH and Mary Eldridge. Surry Co.   C. p.9

30 Apr. 1835 - Robert N. BOOTH and Marietta E. Meade at R. K. Meade's
Brunswick Co. B. p. 305

30 July 1791 - John BOTTOM and Mary Hunnicutt. Sussex Co. C. p.13

24 Oct. 1878 - Thos. Castleman BOURDEN and Lucy C. Thweatt at Res. of
Bride's mother. Dinwiddie Co.   B. p.333

23 Feb. 1798 - John BOWERS and Betsy Bowers. Lunenburg Co. C. p.16

20 Oct. 1803 - Alexander BOYD and Matilda Burwell. Mecklenburg Co. C. p.18

22 Nov. 1799 - Richard BOYD and Panthea Burwell. Mecklenburg Co. C. p.16

14 May 1803 - Robert BOYD and Tabitha Walker. Mecklenburg Co. C. p. 18

26 Apr. 1788 - David BRADLEY and Sally Lessenberry. Prince George Co.
C. p.8

4

17 Sept. 1833 - D. Wilson BRAGG and Roberta C. P. Gilliam at Mrs. Gilliam's, Brunswick Co.   B. p. 304

4 Nov. 1786 - Aaron BRANDOM and Sylvia Lewis. Petersburg. C. p. 5

4 Nov. 1835 - John A. BRANDER and Matilda C. Pegram at Capt. Edward L. Pegram's, Diniiddie Co., B. p. 305

5 Apr. 1836 - James T. BRATTON and Jane R. Lubbock. Prince George Co.M.B.

1 May 1833 - Richard BRISTOW and Ann N. Harmon at Mrs. Nancy Rives', Dinwiddie Co.   B. p. 303

12 May 1802 - Samuel BROADNAX and Margaret B. Holmes. Nottoway Co. C. p. 18

22 Dec. 1837 - Edward BROCKWELL and Frances E. Harris. Prince George Co.

13 Jan. 1838 - John BROCKWELL and Mary Livesay. Prince George Co. M.B.

25 Dec. 1824 - Joseph BROCKWELL and Martha Moore. Prince George Co. M.B.

12 Aug. 1828 - Pleasant BROCKWELL and Patsy Livesay. Prince George Co. M.

15 Feb. 1826 - Samuel BROCKWELL and Nanny J. Williams. Prince George Co. M

12 Dec. 1785 - Thomas BROCKWELL and Jemimah Williams. Prince George Co. C. p. 3

15 Feb. 1834 - William BROCKWELL and Catharine H. Livesay. Prince George Co. M.B.

1 Feb. 1836 - William BROCKWELL and Elizabeth Susan Beeglesten. Prince George Co. M.B.

2 Sept. 1787 - James BROMLEY and Margaret Falkner. Petersburg. C. p. 6

9 May 1849 - Joseph N. BROOKS and Elizabeth Y. Moody. Married by Rev. I. E. Hargrave. Dinwiddie Co. Deed Book 6 p. 191

28 Jan. 1790 - Jeremiah BROWDER and Susannah Clements. Dinwiddie Co. C. p. 11

23 May 1784 - Dudley BROWN and Anne Todd. Dinwiddie Co. C. p. 1

1 Aug. 1784 - Hezekiah BROWN and Tobitha Irby. Dinwiddie Co. C. p. 1

22 Jan. 1789 - John BROWN and Elizabeth Harrison. Prince George Co. C. p. 10

18 Apr. 1831 - Lodowick BROWN and Mary Sturdivant. Prince George Co. M.B.

21 July 1829 - James C. BRUCE and Elisa D. Wilkins at William Wilkins'
Northampton Co., N. C.   B. p. 301

3 Apr. 1805 - Charles BRYDIE and Jane F. Billups. Lunenburg Co. C. p. 18

29 May 1788 - David BUCHANAN and Elizabeth Gilliam. Prince George Co.
C. p. 8

1 June 1837 - Abraham BUFORD and Henrietta A. Hite at Mrs. Mary A. Jones,
Brunswick Co.   B. p. 306

22 Dec. 1808 - Thomas BUFORD and Martha Manson. Nottoway Co. C. p. 19

22 Dec. 1785 - William BURGE and Rebecca Hall. Sussex Co. C. p. 3

12 Jan. 1796 - Richard F. BURKS and Betsey Perkerson. Prince Edward Co.
C. p. 17

3 Dec. 1827 - Henry W. BURROW and Maria P. Williams. Prince George Co. M.B.

14 Oct. 1815 - Henry H. BURWELL and Catharine Buford. Lunenburg Co.
C. p. 20

17 June 1818- William BUSHALL and Elizabeth Edwards (wid.) Prince George Co.M.B.

24 July 1830 - Richard BUTLER and Jane Sheffield. Prince George Co. M.B.

2 Feb. 1836 -James W.E.BUTTS and Virgilla A. HARRISON. Prince George Co.M.B.

18 Dec. 1855 -James M. CABANISS and Martha D. Meredith at Mrs. M. Meredith
B. p. 311

11 July 1831 - Jesse CALDWELL, alias COLVIN, and Mima Seegood. Prince
George Co. M.B.

6 Aug. 1791 - Joseph CALVIN and Elizabeth Wells. Chesterfield Co. C. p. 13

17 Dec. 1791 - Donald CAMERON and Mary Anderson. Prince George Co. C.p.13

21 Dec. 1797 - Ewen CAMERON and Frances Buford. Lunenburg Co. C. p. 17

22 Oct. 1786 - George CAMERON and Elizabeth Hattaway. Petersburg.C.p.5

19 July 1831 - John A. CARSLEY and Elizabeth Moore. Prince George Co. M.B.

17 May 1785 - John CARTER and Ursella Pennington. Sussex Co. C. p. 2

30 Jan. 1805 - Raleigh CARTER and Susanna Stokes. Lunenburg Co. C. p. 18

6 Aug. 1785 - Thomas CARTER and Anne Broadnax. Prince George Co. C. p. 2

17 Dec. 1795 - William CARTER and Jane Crenshaw. Nottoway Co. C. p. 17

22 Dec. 1788 - William M. CARTER and Elizabeth Weeks. Prince George Co. C. p. 9

24 Dec. 1836 - Jesse CARTWRIGHT and Elizabeth Adeline Brown. Prince George Co. M.B.

1 Feb. 1787 - John CATE and Winney Meachum. Sussex Co. C. p. 5

14 July 1787 - James CATTLE and Martha Butler. Petersburg. C. p. 6

31 Mar. 1827 - William F. CHAMBLISS and Mrs. Eliza A. Withers at her house Sussex Co. B. p. 300

13 Dec. 1786 - John CHAPMAN and Margaret Hogan. Petersburg. . C. p. 5

2 July 1812 - John C. CHAPPELL and Milly T. Sandys. Lunenburg Co. C. p.

10 Feb. 1785 - Joel CHEAVES and Sarah Sturdivant. Prince George Co. C. p

20 Apr. 1836 - Dr. Devereux J. CLAIBORNE and Mrs. Martha Lewis. Brunswick Co. B. p. 305

21 Dec. 1791 - Matthew M. CLAIBORNE and Ann Carter Harrison. Sussex Co. C. p. 13

17 Dec. 1890 -James H. CLARK and Susie T. Hawkins at Res. of Thos. C. Hawkins. B. p. 337

8 Nov. 1883 - John Archer CLARK and Anna Gill at Res. of Chas. Gill, Dinwiddie Co. B. p. 334

25 Dec. 1790 - William CLARK and Mary Ann Hare. Chesterfield. C. p. 12

30 Oct. 1837 - George E. CLARKE and Margaret Williams. Prince George M.B.

4 Dec. 1787 - John M. CLARREN and Martha Berry. Chesterfield Co. C. p. 7

24 June 1790 - Thomas CLAYTON and Mary Smith. Chesterfield Co. C. p. 11

26 Jan. 1786 -William CLEMENTS and Anne McCullock. Dinwiddie Co. C.p.3

14 July 1824 - Joseph B. COCKE and Mary E. Gary (Spinster). Prince George M

6 Jan. 1791 - William COGBILL and Elizabeth Covington. Chesterfield Co. C. p. 12

10 Sept. 1840 - Robert COLEMAN, Jr. and Sarah Holloway. Prince George M.B.

11 Dec. 1833 - John R. COLE and Mary H. WILLIAMS. Prince George M. B.

14 Apr. 1796 - Green COLEMAN and Betsy Watkins. Nottoway Co. C. p. 17

18 Aug. 1791 - Nathaniel COLLEY and Martha Jones. Prince George Co. C. p

7

22 Feb. 1787 - David W. COLLIER and Patty Williams. Dinwiddie Co. C. p.6

15 Feb. 1826 - Edward COMER and Christianna Downing. Prince George Co. M.B.

5 Jan. 1822 - James COMER and Barbara Marks (widow). Prince George Co. M.B.

13 Aug. 1828 - William B. COMER and Elizabeth Stafford. Prince George Co. M.B.

17 Apr. 1790 - Benjamin COOK and Mary Blakely. Petersburg. C. p. 11

14 Jan. 1792 - Benjamin COOK and Melinda Cosby. Petersburg. C. p. 14

20 Jan. 1802 - Thomas T. COOKE and Lucy W. Nicholson. Nottoway Co. C. p.18

27 Aug. 1785 - Edmund COOPER and Elizabeth Hodges. Petersburg. C.p.2

18 Dec. 1787 - Richard W. COOPER and Priscilla Inglish. Petersburg. C. p. 7

12 July 1832 - Thomas K. CORNICH and Martha L. MOODY. Prince George Co. M.B.

30 Dec. 1786 - William COSBY and Millender Holsey. Petersburg. C.p.5

20 Aug. 1789 - Hardy COTTON and Patty Saunders. Sussex Co. C. p. 10

31 May 1787 - John COTTON and Celia Lee. Prince George Co. C. p. 6

13 Dec. 1792 - Cary COTTON and Nancy Harrison. Sussex Co. C. p. 14

12 July 1810 - William B. COWAN and Catharine G. Epes. Nottoway Co. C.p.19

27 Aug. 1846 - Dr. William COLE and Clara H. Peter at the Res. of Mrs. Margaret B. Wyatt, Meherrin Par., Greenville Co. B. p.309

16 Jan. 1794 - George COX and Mary Friend. Chesterfield Co. C. p. 15

11 July 1805 - George CRAIG and Anne W. Chambers. Lunenburg Co. C. p. 18

30 Apr. 1851 - Dr. James R. CRAIG and Lucy Ann Bolling, both of Dinwiddie Co. B. p. 311

3 Dec. 1795 - Richard Kenner CRALLE and Sarah Jones. Lunenburg Co. C.p.17

29 June 1808 - William CRALLE and Sally Jones. Nottoway Co. C. p. 19

15 Dec. 1792 - Michael CRASMUCH and Elizabeth Barlow. Petersburg. C.p.14

1 Feb. 1822 - James M. CREIGHTON and Miriam Sears (Spinster) Prince George M.B.

20 Feb. 1786 - John CRIDER and Mildred Hobbs. Prince George. C. p. 3

22 Feb. 1797 - Richard CROSS and Sally Chambers. Lunenburg Co. C. p.17

20 Feb. 1834 - Richard D. CROSS and Elizabeth B. Wells at Mr. Samuel Wells, Dinwiddie Co. B. p. 304

11 Dec. 1832 – John P. CRUMP and Susan W. Wynn at Dr. Copland's, Dinwiddie Co. B. p. 303

25 Nov. 1833 – George W. CUMMINGS and Elizabeth Stackhouse. Prince George Co. M.B.

19 Sept. 1836 – William CUMMINGS and Jane Hite. Prince George Co. M.B.

7 Sept. 1785 – William CUNNINGHAM and Obedience Hacker. Petersburg. C. p. 2

15 Sept. 1803 – Ellyson CURRIE and Anne Gilliam. Petersburg. C.p.18

23 Dec. 1840 – George W. CURTIS and Mary Ann Folkes. Prince George Co. M

20 May 1833 – Edmund H. DANIEL and Sarah L. Peebles. Issued in Sussex Co. Prince George Co. M.B.

17 Dec. 1789 – John Holloway DANIEL and Nancy Davenport. Prince George C. p. 11

22 Jan. 1835 – Thomas DANIEL and Elizabeth D. Newell. Prince George Co. M

6 Dec. 1792 – Thomas DANIEL and Lucretia Deahart. Prince George Co. C.p.

24 Dec. 1787 – Joseph DAVENPORT and Judith Richardson. Petersburg C. p.

9 Apr. 1786 – John DAVIS and Susanna Swepson. Mecklenburg Co. C. p. 4

22 Jan. 1811 – Samuel D. DAVIES and Mary N. Stout. Lunenburg Co. C. p.20

19 Nov. 1785 – Shepherd DAVIS and Martha Williams. Prince George Co. C. p. 2

11 Mar. 1789 – William DAVIS and Mason Hardaway. Dinwiddie Co. C. p. 10

16 Sept. 1809 – Boswell B. De-GRAFFENREID and Frances Garland. Lunenburg Co. C. p. 19

2 Apr. 1785 – Samuel DEMOVILL and Elizabeth Taylor Eppes. Prince George Co C. p. 2

19 Feb. 1789 – Shadrack DENHART and Lettice McDowell. Prince George Co. C. p. 10

5 Feb. 1791 – James DINTON and Winefred Alley. Prince George Co. C. p.12

19 Jan. 1793 – Drury DISHMAN and Margaret Totty. Chesterfield Co. C.p.15

12 Feb. 1787 – Robert DIXON and Joannah Thrift. Prince George Co. C. p.6

9 Dec. 1786 – Joseph DOUGHERTY and Letty Macken. Prince George Co. C. p.5

11 Aug. 1787 - Alexander DRAYNAN and Mary Ann Murphy. Prince George Co. C. p. 6

8 Nov. 1832 - Rev. Charles DRESSER and Louisa W. Withers at Mr. Thomas Withers', Dinwiddie Co. B. p. 303

3 Apr. 1828 - William H. DUELL and Mahala Clarke, (Spinster) Prince George Co. M.B.

13 July 1786 - Nathaniel DUNN and Betty Thweatt. Prince George Co. C.p.4

19 Feb. 1823 - Richard G. DUNN and Sarah N. Gary (Spinster) Prince George Co. M.B.

17 Apr. 1787 - Thomas DUNN and Lucy Green. Prince George Co. C. p. 6

5 Feb. 1833 - Dr. Joel W. DUPUY and Paulina B. Eldridge at Mrs. Sally Edmonds', Brunswick Co. B. p. 303

13 June 1826 - John DURANT and Sarah Hodge (widow) Prince George M.B.

1 Nov. 1787 - Daniel DYSON and Jinny Gill. Chesterfield Co. C. p. 6

23 Jan. 1790 - John EANES and Margaret DODD. Chesterfield Co. C. p. 11

15 Feb. 1831 - Sterling F. EDMUNDS and Ann J. Cocke. Prince George Co. M.B.

28 Jan. 1787 - Stephen EDWARDS and Elizabeth Watts. Prince George Co. C.p.5

18 Dec. 1798 - Henry S. ELLIS and Sally D. Pettus. Lunenburg. C. p. 16

17 Jan. 1848 - James F. ELLYSON and Jane A.E. Roffe. Married by Rev. I. E. Hargrave, M.E. Church, South. Dinwiddie Co. Deed Book 6 p. 191

5 Dec. 1831 - Thomas EMORY and Mary Stainback. Prince George Co. M.B.

26 Sept. 1799 - Francis EPES and Sarah G. Williams. Nottoway Co. C.p.16

21 Jan. 1802 - John EPES and Frances H. Campbell. Nottoway Co. C. p.18

4 Nov. 1807 - John EPES and Mary Ann Wells. Nottoway Co. C. p. 19

15 Feb. 1798 - Peter EPES and Rebecca Cross. Lunenburg Co. C. p. 16

10 July 1800 - Richard EPES and Martha G. Williams. Nottoway Co. C. p.16

11 Oct. 1830 - Robert F. EPES and Mary R. Marks. Prince George Co. M.B.

9 Dec. 1786 - William EPES and Patience Morison. Prince George Co. C.p.5

2 Jan. 1833 - Daniel EPPES and Phoebe Moody. Prince George Co. M.B.

14 Dec. 1825 - Francis EPPES and Ann Donaldson (widow) Prince George M.B.

7 Jan. 1835 - John T. EPPES and Ann Hackney. Prince George Co. M.B.

31 July 1788 - Temple EPPES and Nancy Temple. Prince George Co. C. p.9

21 April 1831 - Thomas EPPES and Jane Allen (alias Harrison) Prince George Co. M.B.

29 April 1830 - Batty H. EVANS and Ann H. Young at Charles Young's, Dinwiddie Co. B. p. 302

21 Jan. 1786 - Buckner EZELL and Elizabeth Birckett. Prince George Co. C.p

24 Mar. 1787 - John M. FARQUHAR and Frances Vaughan. Dinwiddie Co. C.p.6

19 Jan. 1790 - William FASON and Elizabeth Stainback. Prince George Co. C. p. 11

23 Oct. 1828 - Dr. John FEILD and Mary H. Bolling at Mrs. Mary Bolling's, Dinwiddie Co. B. p. 301

25 Dec. 1788 - William FERGUSON and Rebecca Patterson. Prince George Co. C. p. 9

14 Jan. 1825 - Robert FEWQUA and Pamila Titmash, Spinster, Prince George Co. M.B.

1 Aug. 1822 - James FEWQUA and Martha A. E. Blackwell, Spinster, Prince George Co. M.B.

10 Oct. 1791 - Alexander S. FIELD and Jane Stewart. Prince George Co. C. p. 13

28 Feb. 1787 - Theophilus FIELD and Susan Thweatt. Prince George Co. C.p.6

3 Sept. 1828 - Thomas I. FIRTH and Sarah Hawkins at Phillip Hawkins', Dinwiddie Co. B. p. 300

8 Nov. 1787 - John Ravenscroft FISHER and Elizabeth Wily. Prince George Co. C. p. 7

3 Apr. 1855 - Edmund O. FITZGERALD and Susan J. Gilliam, at Res. of her mother. B. p. 311

4 Nov. 1805 - Francis FITZGERALD and Frances Jones. Nottoway Co. C. p.18

21 Aug. 1794 - Francis FITZGERALD and Catharine Ward. Nottoway Co. C. p.17

20 Dec. 1810 - Thomas FITZGERALD and Ann R. Williams. Nottoway Co. C.p.19

21 Nov. 1833 - Matthew M. FLETCHER and Martha H. Scott at Col. James Scott's, Dinwiddie Co. B. p. 304

7 Mar. 1805 - Nathan FLETCHER and Mary Nicholson. Nottoway Co. C. p. 18

22 Jan. 1789 - Jeremiah FORD and Nancy Draper. Prince George Co. C. p. 10

7 Aug. 1785 - Seth FOSTER and Anne King. Prince George Co. C. p. 2

24 Nov. 1836 - Xavier S. FOSTER and Lucy Ann Ledbetter, at Garduer Ledbetter's, Dinwiddie Co. B. p. 305

18 Dec. 1855 - D. H. FRAHER and A. E. Johnson, at Res. of Mr. Ben Johnson, Brunswick Co. B. p. 311

12 Mar. 1788 - Alexander FRANKLYN and Anne Hoy. Chesterfield Co. C. p.8

Feb. Court 1789 - Alexander FRASER and Dicey Shackleford. (Marriage Contract) Dinwiddie Co. Order Book 1789-1791, Page 4.

23 Sept. 1785 - John FREEMAN and Milly Heath. Prince George Co. C. p.2

13 Nov. 1821 - William T. GALT and Elizabeth Lany (widow) Prince George Co. M.B.

22 Jan. 1789 - Benjamin GARY and Mary Underhill. Sussex Co. C. p. 10

17 Dec. 1823 - George G. GARY and Pamela Gary (Spinster) Prince George Co. M.B.

13 June 1793 - Hartwell GARY and Rebecca Butterworth. Prince George Co. C. p. 15

5 Mar. 1786 - John GARY and Sally Weaver. Sussex Co. C. p. 3

1 Apr. 1792 - Richard GARY and Mary Bonner. Prince George Co. C. p. 14

10 Jan. 1788 - Thomas GARY and Elizabeth Proctor. Prince George Co. C. p. 8

12 Dec. 1787 - Charles GEE and Susannah Peebles. Sussex Co. C. p. 7

10 June 1830 - James L. GEE and Julia Ann Backus. Prince George Co. M.B.

17 Dec. 1788 - John GEE and Judith Rives. Prince George Co. C. p. 9

30 Apr. 1789 - James GEDDY, Jr. and Euphan Armistead. Petersburg. C.p.10

6 July 1793 - John GIBBS and Mary Gill. Chesterfield Co. C. p. 15

15 Apr. 1790 - Aaron GILL and Jency Gill. Chesterfield Co. C. p. 11

7 Mar. 1854 - Chas. O. GILL and Susan R. Traylor, both of Dinwiddie Co. at Res. of her grandmother. B. p. 311

19 Feb. 1824 - Chamberlain GILL and Lucy Brown (Spinster). Prince George M.B.

8 June 1786 – Erasmus GILL and Sarah Newsum. Dinwiddie Co. C. p. 4

15 Nov. 1788 – Joseph GILL and Mary Brown. Chesterfield Co. C. p. 9

4 Dec. 1788 – Joseph GILL and Fanny Glassco. Chesterfield Co. C. p. 9

25 Dec. 1788 – Vaden GILL and Elizabeth Granger. Chesterfield Co. C. p.9

7 Feb. 1790 – William GILL and Anne Andross. Chesterfield Co. C. p. 11

21 Nov. 1787 – James Skelton GILLIAM and Mary Field. Prince George Co. C. p. 7

30 Apr. 1789 – William GILLIAM and Christian Eppes. Prince George Co. C. p. 10

12 Dec. 1826 – James B. GILMOUR and Elizabeth H. Folkes. Prince George Co. M.

2 Feb. 1788 – Edward GLOVER and Rebeccah Major. Prince George Co. C. p.

15 Nov. 1788 – George GODFREY and Mary Silvie. Prince George Co. C. p. 9

20 Nov. 1834 – Albert T. GOODWYN and Aurelia Meade, at the Grove, Brunswick Co. B. p. 304

15 Apr. 1786 – James GOODWYN and Frances Lowry Brown. Petersburg. C. p. 4

23 Dec. 1786 – Stephen GOODWYN and Elizabeth Watkins. Dinwiddie Co. C.p.5

5 May 1828 – William B. GOODWYN and Rebecca T. Gill. Prince George Co. M

7 Jan. 1786 – John GOODY and Susanna Cain. Prince George Co. C. p. 3

21 Apr. 1803 – Thomas GORDON and Elizabeth Westmore (widow). Petersburg. C. p. 18

21 Sept. 1803 – Robert GRAHAM and Eliza Lockhead. Lunenburg. C. p. 18

15 Apr. 1826 – Briggs R. GRAMMER and Patsey C. Lanthrope. Prince George M

24 Dec. 1828 – Hartwell E. GRAMMER and Elizabeth Titmash. Prince George Co.

27 Mar. 1790 – James GRAMMER and Nancy Wells. Petersburg. C. p. 11

1 May 1788 – John GRAMMER and Priscilla Withers. Dinwiddie Co. C. p. 8

1 Jan. 1793 – Nathan GRAMMER and Frances Russell. Petersburg. C. p. 15

26 Aug. 1827 – Robert W. GRAMMER and Mrs. Ann Manlove, at her house in. Dinwiddie Co. B. p. 300

17 Feb. 1785 – Sampson GRANTHAM and Elizabeth Mansell Simmons. Sussex Co. C. p. 2

8 Dec. 1837 - Cornelius GRAVES and Eliza Chappell. Prince
George Co. M.B.

8 Jan. 1785 - William GRAY and Maria Randolph. Prince George Co.
C. p. 2

17 Oct. 1805 - Richard C. GREGORY and Frances Craig. Lunenburg Co.
C. p. 18

22 Apr. 1787 - Francis Burwell GREEN and Mary Batte. Prince
George Co. C. p. 6

27 June 1789 - John GREEN and Jane Morison. Prince George Co.
C. p. 10

20 Mar. 1827 - William B. GREEN and Catharine W. Epps at John F.
Epps, Nottoway Co. B. p. 300

15 Feb. 1790 - George GREENHOW and Margaret Granger. Petersburg.
C. p. 11

13 Mar. 1839 - William H. GRIFFITH and Ann M. Wilkinson. Prince
George Co. M.B.

18 June 1785 - Francis HADDON and Becky Raines. Prince George Co.
C. p. 2

5 June 1787 - Joel HALL and Betsey Chambliss. Sussex Co. C. p. 6

25 Dec. 1790 - Edward HALL and Lucy Hardaway. Dinwiddie Co. C.p. 12

10 Sept. 1833 - Robert HALL and Lucy Whitmore. Prince George Co. M.B.

5 May 1818 - William HALL and Sally W. Cummings (Spinster). Prince
George Co. M.B.

18 May 1809 - John HAMLIN and Mary Williams. Lunenburg Co. C. p.19

12 Jan. 1832 - James E. HAMMONS and Martha Evans, at Mr. Richard
Evans', Dinwiddie Co. B. p. 303

23 Dec. 1784 - Thomas HANKS and Margaret Clements. Dinwiddie Co. C.p.1

25 Feb. 1786 - John HARE and Anne Burton. Chesterfield Co. C. p. 3

16 Jan. 1839 - John B. HARRIS and Sarah Hackney. Prince George Co. M.B.

6 Dec. 1825 - Joseph S. HARRIS and Parthena J.A.E. Grantham. Prince
George Co. M.B.

3 July 1787 - Thomas HARRIS and Elizabeth Womack. Prince George
Co. C. p. 6

21 Dec. 1793 - Benjamin HARRISON and Anne Osborne. Prince George Co. C. p. 15

24 Jan. 1788 - Cuthbert HARRISON and Fanny Holt. Chesterfield Co. C. p. 8

12 Sept. 1797 - David HARRISON and Mary Moore. Lunenburg Co. C. p. 17

14 Jan. 1787 - Edmund HARRISON and Mary Murray. Prince George Co. C.p.5

10 Feb. 1791 - Henry HARRISON and Elizabeth Underhill. Sussex Co. C.p.12

4 Mar. 1786 - Josiah HARRISON and Mary Underhill. Sussex Co. C. p. 3

1 Mar. 1791 - Obediah Read HARRISON and Mason Cain. Prince George Co. C.1

28 Dec. 1837 - Peyton HARRISON and Nancy Thomas Phillips. Prince George Co. M. B.

8 Oct. 1839 - Robert HARRISON and Eliza Livesay. Prince George Co. M.B.

6 Dec. 1788 - William HARRISON and Ann Morison. Prince George Co. C. p.9

30 July 1785 - William HART and Anne Stainback. Dinwiddie Co. C. p. 2

31 Mar. 1790 - Peter HARWELL and Betsey Hawthorne. Sussex Co. C. p. 11

31 Dec. 1790 - Christopher HASKINS and Elizabeth Booker. Petersburg C. p. 12

12 Feb. 1789 - George HATCH and Mary Shaw Thompson. Sussex Co. C. p. 10

13 Feb. 1792 - Daniel HATCHER and Mary Walthall. Chesterfield. C. p. 14

16 Jan. 1809 - Archibald HATCHETT and Mary Epes Jones LAMKIN. Lunenburg Co. C. p. 19

4 Aug. 1791 - Thomas HATTON and Anne Redwood. Petersburg. C. p. 13

2 May 1803 - John D. HAWKINS and Jane A. Boyd. Mecklenburg Co. C. p. 18

1 Sept. 1785 - Thomas HAWKINS and Courtney Irvin. Petersburg. C. p. 2

24 Dec. 1803 - William HAWKINS and Nancy Boyd. Mecklenburg Co. C. p. 18

20 Dec. 1848 - Benjamin A. HAWKS and Julia A. P. Pool. Married by Rev. I. E. Hargrave. Dinwiddie Co. Deed Book 6, p. 191

30 Dec. 1786 - Joshua HAWTHORN and Nancy Heth. Prince George Co. C. p.5

20 Sept. 1877 - Harrison J. HEARTWELL and Susan A. Hardaway, at Res. of bride in Dinwiddie Co. B. p. 333

7 May 1786 - Austin HEATH and Sarah Woodleif. Prince George Co. C.p.4

23 Feb. 1788 - Daniel HEATH and Mary Livesay. Prince George Co. C. p.8

7 Mar. 1793 - Frederick HEATH and Judith Rives. Prince George Co. C.p.15

10 Sept. 1833 - Henry G. HEATH and Eliza A. Marks. Prince George Co. M.B.

11 Jan. 1794 - Joseph HEATH and Ede Williams. Prince George Co. C.p.15

30 Jan. 1788 - Nathan HEATH and Elizabeth Dunn. Sussex Co. C. p. 8

4 Nov. 1787 - Michael HEATHCOTE and Mary Wily. Petersburg. C. p. 6

21 June 1788 - Jonathan HERBERT and Nanny Wilkins. Prince George Co.
C. p. 8

24 Sept. 1786 - Jesse HERRING and Anne Woodleif. Prince George Co.
C. p. 4

16 Sept. 1790 - Jesse HETH and Agnes Peebles. Prince George Co. C.p.11

27 Dec. 1787 - William HETH and Rebeccah Young. Dinwiddie Co. C. p. 7

20 Dec. 1837 - Col. Robert C. HILLIARD and Mary R. H. Walker, at
Capt. Jno. Jones, Brunswick Co.   B. p. 306

2 June 1835 - John HITE and Eliza Eppes. Prince George Co. M.B.

18 Oct. 1831 - John W. HITE and Martha Williams. Prince George Co. M.B.

21 Dec. 1838 - Wilie HITE and Alivia Ann Hackney. Prince George Co. M.B.

24 Dec. 1822 - Allen HOBBS and Mary Hite (Spinster) Prince George Co.M.B.

18 Dec. 1837 - Herbert W. HOBBS and Mariah P. Burrow. Prince George
Co. M.B.

23 Dec. 1831 - Holloway HOBBS and Rebecca C. Rives. Prince George Co. M.B.

29 Jan. 1789 - Isham HOBBS and Elizabeth Clark. Sussex Co. C. p. 10

18 Apr. 1837 - Joseph M. HOBBS and Sarah Jones. Prince George Co. M.B.

17 Feb. 1818 - William HOCKNEY and Sally W. Womack (Spinster). Prince
George Co. M.B.

7 Nov. 1786 - Edmund HOLLIDAY and Elizabeth Chapel. Petersburg. C.p.5

30 Oct. 1790 - John HOOD and Elizabeth Osborne Downman. Chesterfield
Co. C. p.12

9 Feb. 1831 - William H. HOOD and Susan Perkinson. Prince George Co. M.B.

28 Feb. 1792 - George HOUSE and Ann Wells. Chesterfield Co. C. p. 14

1 Oct. 1829 - Richard HOWERTON and Martha Emily Bolling, at Mrs. Mary Bolling's, Dinwiddie Co. B. p. 301

20 May 1786- James HOWLE and Pamelia Tyus. Sussex Co. C. p. 4

9 Nov. 1824 - Ephraim HUNNICUTT and Rachel Hunnicut. Prince George Co. M.

8 Dec. 1785 - Pleasant HUNNICUTT and Mary Cocke. Sussex Co. C. p. 3

29 May 1879 - Thomas HUNT of Sussex Co. and Roberta Heartwell, at Res. of H. J. Heartwell. B. p. 333

22 Dec. 1787 - Miles HUNTER and Martha Pritchard. Petersburg. C. p. 7

20 Jan. 1788 - Thomas Tod HUNTER and Alice Harrison. Prince George Co. C. p. 8

18 Mar. 1834 - James M. HURT and Elizabeth D. Davis, at A. S. Lockhead's, Lawrenceville. B. p. 304

5 Jan. 1786- George IVY and Amelia Peterson. Prince George Co. C. p. 3

22 Dec. 1789 - Ezekiel JACKSON and Rhode Dance. Chesterfield Co. C. p.11

15 Dec. 1785 - William JACKSON and Sally Eckles. Sussex Co. C.p.3

11 Jan. 1789 - Daniel JAMESON and Polly Watts. Prince George Co. C. p.10

7 Sept. 1786 - John JEFFRIES and Anne Elizabeth Jones. Chesterfield Co. C.p

7 Aug. 1827 - Alexander JOHNSON and Elizabeth Moore. Prince George Co. M.

18 Dec. 1827 - Edward JOHNSON and Minerva Stith, at Mrs. Jane Stith's, Brunswick Co. B. p. 300

20 Mar. 1788 - John JOHNSON and Alley Peterson. Prince George Co. M.B.

7 Jan. 1787 - Abraham JOHNSTON and Sukey Tench. Prince George Co. C. p.5

17 Sept. 1840 - Sampson JOHNSTON and Ann Brockwell. Prince George Co. M.B.

29 Dec. 1831 - Archibald JOLLY and Elizabeth Perkins. "In my own study at 1/2 past 12 o'clock A.M." B. p. 302

6 Oct. 1796 - Lewellyn JONES and Prudence Ward. Amelia Co. C. p. 17

1 Sept. 1798 - Littleberry H. JONES and Elizabeth Fitzgerald. Nottoway Co C. p. 16

13 May 1806 - Peter B. JONES and Martha Epes. Nottoway Co. C. p. 18

2 June 1807 - Peter JONES, Jr. and Sally G. Bacon. Lunenburg Co. C.p.19

6 Aug. 1785 - Philip JONES and Martha Erskine. Prince George Co. C. p. 2

2 July 1795 - Richard JONES and Mary Ellis. Nottoway Co. C. p. 17

15 June 1786 -Thomas Brooks JONES and Rebeccah Edwards Jones. Chesterfield Co. C. p. 4

23 Feb. 1826 -Thomas W. JONES and Pamela A. Comer (Spinster). Prince George Co. M.B.

3 Jan. 1804 - Baxter JORDAN and Polly L. Pettus. Lunenburg Co. C. p. 18

20 Nov. 1804 - Miles JORDAN and Harriott Pettus. Mecklenburg Co. C. p.18

1 Nov. 1802 - Samuel JORDAN and Jean Scott. Lunenburg Co. C. p. 18

21 July 1789 - John KELLY and Elizabeth Holden. Petersburg. C. p. 10

12 Mar. 1790 - John KENT and Elizabeth K. Halsey. Dinwiddie Co. C. p. 11

12 Sept. 1832 - George KERR and Ann Moran (widow). Petersburg. B. p. 303

8 Mar. 1788 - Mark KILLINGSWORTH and Charlotte Caleb. Prince George Co. C. p. 8

13 Apr. 1887 -Charles A. KING and Sarah V. T. Wells, at Sapony Church B. p. 335

19 July 1799 - Miles KING and Frances Powell Burwell. Mecklenburg Co. C. p. 16

8 Dec. 1792 - Bartley KIRKLAND and Lucy Grammer. Prince George Co. C.p.14

20 May 1790 - John KIRKLAND and Agness Lee. Petersburg. C. p. 11

11 Apr. 1787 - John Brownlow KNOX and Elizabeth Jones. Petersburg. C.p.6

8 Dec. 1787 - Thomas B. LACEY and Frances Hopkins. Petersburg. C. p. 7

16 Dec. 1835 - Abner W. LANIER and Susan E. Feild, at Mr. Burwell B. Wilkes', Brunswick Co. B. p. 305

7 Jan. 1789 - John LANIER and Catherine Fallett. Prince George Co. C.p.10

31 Jan. 1786 - William LANTHROP and Susannah Davenport. Prince George Co. C. p. 3

7 Sept. 1825 - Jesse LANTHROPE and Mary A. Temple. Prince George Co. M.B.

31 Dec. 1789 - Leadbetter LANTHOUPE and Lucretia Livesay. Prince George Co. C. p. 11

21 Feb. 1788 - Edward LEE and Polly Bonner. Prince George Co. C. p. 8

_ Dec. 1824 - Henry LEE and Lucy Lesenbery. Prince George Co. M.B.

13 Dec. 1792 - Herbert LEE and Lucy Daniel. Prince George Co. C. p. 14

23 Dec. 1788 - Jesse LEE and Elizabeth Williams. Prince George Co. C.p.

7 Oct. 1790 - John Taylor LEE and Sarah Chappell Moore. Prince George Co
C. p. 12

30 Aug. 1792 - Matthew LEE and Elizabeth Crowder. Dinwiddie Co. C. p. 14

18 Sept. 1806 - David G. LEIGH and Mary B. Stevenson. Lunenburg Co. C.p.1

28 Nov. 1793 - John LeMESSURIER and Frances Bolling. Petersburg C. p. 15

23 Nov. 1786 - Joseph LENOX and Nellie Field. Petersburg. C. p. 5

22 Oct. 1848 - John B. LEWIS and Mary J. Wells, married by Rev. I. E.
Hargrave. Dinwiddie Co. Deed Book 6 p. 191

11 Nov. 1788 - Robert LEWIS and Anne Bugg. Mecklenburg Co. C. p. 9

11 Dec. 1879 - William H. LEWIS and Catherine Abernathy, at Res. of Charle
Gill, Dinwiddie Co. B. p. 333

24 Dec. 1785 - Burwell LIVESAY and Frankey Grammer. Prince George Co.
C. p. 3

20 Jan. 1791 - Thomas LIVESAY and Ann Womack. Prince George Co. C. p. 12

2 Nov. 1793 - Thomas LIVESAY and Sally Livesay. Prince George Co. C.p.15

1 Feb. 1832 - Wilson LIVESAY and Milly Livesay. Prince George Co. M.B.

8 Nov. 1798 - Allan LOVE and Mary Edmunds. Brunswick Co. C. p. 16

21 Aug. 1796 - Thomas LOWRY and Martha A. Stevenson. Lunenburg Co. C.p.1

20 Dec. 1882 - Thaddeus C. LUCY and Augusta Thrift, at Res. of Thomas M.
Thrift, Dinwiddie Co. B. p. 334

18 Oct. 1786 - Henry LYNCH and Eleanor M. Donnell. Petersburg. C. p.4

14 Apr. 1787 - John MacFARLAN and Frances Williamson. Petersburg. C.p.6

25 Jan. 1830 - Alexander D. McBROOM and Maria Frances Daniel. Prince
George Co. M.B.

19 Dec. 1817 - Thomas McCANN and Poline Stevens (Spinster). Prince George
Co. M.B.

16 Jan. 1794 - John McDOWELL and Mary Duran. Petersburg. C. p. 15

30 Mar. 1790 - Alexander McKEEVER and Sally Jones. Chesterfield Co. C.p.11

9 Feb. 1793 - David McKITTRICK and Obedience Cunningham. Petersburg C.p.15

25 Dec. 1793 - Neil McLAREN and Elizabeth Andrews. Petersburg. C. p. 15

25 July 1787 - Daniel McLAURIN and Susannah Edwards. Chesterfield Co.
C. p. 6

27 Apr. 1786 - John McLEOD and Isabella Hamilton. Prince George Co. C.p.4

6 Dec. 1789 - Robert MACKY and Ann Bradley. Petersburg. C. p. 10

25 Oct. 1788 - David MAITLAND and Susanna Poythress. Prince George Co.
C. p. 9

21 Dec. 1793 - William MAITLAND and Elizabeth Eppes. Prince George Co.
C. p. 15

15 Dec. 1785 - William MAJOR and Susanna Williams. Dinwiddie Co. C. p. 3

8 April 1830 - Joseph E. MANLOVE and Winifred G. Mitchell, at Jacob
Mitchell's, Sussex Co. B. p. 302

9 Jan. 1794 - George MARABLE and Rebeccah Williams. Prince George Co.
C. p. 15

29 Aug. 1840 - Christopher MARKS and Harriet Livesay. Prince George Co.M.B.

14 June 1792 - John MARKS and Martha Lanier. Dinwiddie Co. C. p. 14

19 May 1829 - John C. MARKS and Susan E. L. Price. Issued in Surry Co.
Surety: Ephriam Simmons. Prince George Co. M.B.

23 Dec. 1819 - Lewis MARKS and Polly Marks (Spinster). Prince George Co.M.B.

15 Dec. 1817 - Richard MARKS and Elizabeth B. Poythress (Spinster). Prince
George Co. M.B.

8 Jan. 1835 - William R. MARKS and Mary S. Fewqua. Prince George Co. M.B.

6 Mar. 1786 - Smallwood Coghill MARLOW and Mildred Flack. Petersburg.
C. p. 3

17 July 1787 - Alexander MARSHALL and Anne Walthall. Chesterfield Co.
C. p. 6

20 Nov. 1850 - William N. MARTIN and Virginia H. Newbill, at Res. of
her Brother, Dinwiddie Co. B. p. 310

2 Mar. 1836 - Dr. George MASON and Lucy B. Jones, at Mrs. Mary A. Jones', Brunswick Co. B. p. 305

27 Jan. 1791 - John MASON and Lucy Massenburg. Sussex Co. C. p. 12

28 Mar. 1799 - John R. MASON and Sarah H. Cargill. Brunswick Co. C. p.16

8 Dec. 1840 - Rishworth MASON and Lucy Ann Moody. Prince George Co. M.B.

21 Dec. 1826 - Dr. Robert MASON and Susan G. Cutler, at Dr. Cutler's, Dinwiddie Co. B. p. 300

31 Jan. 1789 - Robert MASSENBURG and Mary Jones. Dinwiddie Co. C. p. 10

29 Jan. 1801 - Robert Clinton MASTERS and Rebecca Tarry. Lunenburg Co. C. p. 16

20 July 1829 - John MATTOX and Lucy B. Green. Prince George Co. M.B.

12 Feb. 1829 - David MAY and Maria Ward Pegram, at Gen. Pegram's, Dinwiddie Co. B. p. 301

10 Dec. 1816 - Henry MEACHEN and Mary W. Comer (Spinster). Prince George Co. M.B.

24 Dec. 1789 - Jeremiah MEACHAM and Milly Cate. Prince George Co. C. p.

17 July 1833 - John A. MEADE and Eliza Jane Turnbull, at Mr. Ro. Turnbull Brunswick Co. B. p. 304

19 Sept. 1832 - Theophilus MEADE and Susan E. Haskins, at R. K. Mead's, Brunswick Co. B. p. 303

3 Apr. 1828 - James Addison MEANLY and Mary Ann Jolly, at Richard Meanly' Dinwiddie Co. B. p. 300

27 Jan. 1886 - J. W. MERRIMON and M. E. Abernathy, at Res. of Mr. Charles Gill, B. p. 335

2 Mar. 1830 - James MILBY and Sally C. Conaway. Prince George Co. M.B.

19 Oct. 1848 - Robert MINETREE and Elizabeth Lewis. Married by Rev. I. E Hargrave. Dinwiddie Co. Deed Book 6, p. 191

18 Aug. 1791 - George MITCHELL and Rebecca Livesay. Prince George Co. C. p. 13

3 Feb. 1791 - Robert MITCHELL and Celah Smith. Prince George Co. C. p.1

2 Jan. 1793 - Benjamin MONTGOMERY and Sarah Cook. Sussex Co. C. p. 15

16 Dec. 1833 - Benjamin MOORE and Martha A. M. Spain. Prince George Co.M.

20 Feb. 1828 - Gilliam R. MOORE and Elizabeth Emery (Spinster). Prince George Co. M.B.

24 Nov. 1787 - James MOORE and Martha Williams. Prince George Co. C.p.7

8 Feb. 1825 - Uriah MOORE and Ann Elizabeth Williams (Spinster). Prince George Co. M.B.

15 Oct. 1786 - Charles MORGAN and Rebeccah Thompson. Prince George Co. C. p. 4

24 June 1786 - Maurice MORIARTY and Judy Hammond. Petersburg. C. p. 4

27 Mar. 1790 - George MORISON and Mary Gracie. Petersburg. C. p. 11

14 June 1798 - John MORRISON and Mary Chappel Bagley. Lunenburg Co. C. p. 16

26 Dec. 1786 - David MOSELY and Amey Finn. Prince George Co. C. p. 5

7 Jan. 1792 - John MOSLEY and Nancy Folks. Chesterfield Co. C. p. 14

28 July 1785 - Henry MOSS and Kesiah Freeman. Sussex Co. C. p. 2

11 Apr. 1787 - Edward MURPHEY and Elizabeth Kerr. Petersburg. C. p. 6

26 May 1785 - Martin MURPHY and Rebeckah Russell. Petersburg. C. p. 2

27 Mar. 1788 - Edward NEWALL and Lucy Lanier. Prince George Co. C.p.8

26 Dec. 1787 - James NEWALL and Jemimah Leath. Prince George Co. C.p.7

9. Apr. 1811 - Henry NEWBILL and Jane Moore. Lunenburg Co. C. p. 20

30 Dec. 1785 - Henry NICHOLL and Frances Hackney. Prince George Co. C. p. 3

15 Sept. 1829 - John Y. NICHOLSON and Sarah B. Moody. Prince George M.B.

20 Feb. 1839 - John NICKLE and Lucretia White. Prince George Co. M.B.

3 June 1786 - William NICKOLS and Nancy Park. Petersburg. C. p. 4

31 Oct. 1829 - John NORRIS and Ann Fisher. Prince George Co. M.B.

15 Dec. 1789 - James NORTHINGTON and Martha Chappell. Prince George Co. C. p. 10

13 Mar. 1833 - Pleasant NUNNALLY and Lucy A. Perkinson. Prince George Co. M.B.

27 Aug. 1785 - Nathaniel NUNNELLY and Polly Andrews. Dinwiddie Co. C. p. 2

8 Feb. 1787 - Augustine OGBURN and Elizabeth Massenburg. Sussex Co. C.p.5

8 Feb. 1787 - Nicholas OGBURN and Mary Harrison. Sussex Co. C. p. 5

9 May 1804 - Isaac OLIVER and Mary A.G. Bacon. Lunenburg Co. C. p.18

21 Jan. 1862 - Edwyn Henry ORGAIN and Paulona Goodwyn, at Res. of Mrs. Goodwyn. B. p. 331

16 June 1792 - Francis OSBORNE and Anne Turnbull. Prince George Co. C. p. 14

2 May 1793 - John OSBORNE and Jane Pleasant Harrison. Prince George Co. C. p. 15

22 Dec. 1787 - Edmund OWEN and Sarah Rives. Prince George Co. C. p. 7

2 Jan. 1789 - William OXLEY and Elizabeth McLaughlan. Prince George Co. C. p. 10

29 Sept. 1785 - Halcott PALMOUR and Effee Epes. Prince George Co. C.p.2

25 -Nov. 1834 - William T. PARHAM and Sarah E. Maclin. Greensville Co. M.R. 1781-1853 p. 117 and B. p. 304

20 Sept. 1785 - Antonio Lee PARK and Betty Cain. Prince George Co. C.p.2

25 Sept. 1817 - William PATTON and Critty Womack (Spinster). Prince George Co. M.B.

29 Sept. 1785 - James PEEBLES and Elizabeth Atkins Rives. Prince George Co. C. p. 2

26 Nov. 1835 - Robert B. PEGRAM and Lucy B. Cargill, at Col. Cargill's, Sussex Co. B. p. 305

20 June 1888 - David B. PERKINS and Lucy H. Gill, at Sapony Church B.p.336

31 Jan. 1788 - Lewis PERKINS and Leah Moody. Prince George Co. C. p. 8

17 Sept. 1829 - Samuel PERKINS and Mary Aspey. Prince George Co. M.B.

18 Oct. 1848 - William S. PERKINS and Mary E. A. Perkins. Married by Rev. I. E. Hargrave. Dinwiddie Co. Deed Book 6, p. 191

13 Dec. 1787 - Daniel PERKINSON and Mary Mann. Chesterfield Co. C. p. 7

17 Nov. 1792 - Field PERKINSON and Pricilla Perkinson. Chesterfield Co. C. p. 14

13 Apr. 1793 - Francis PERKINSON and Frances Andrews. Chesterfield Co. C. p. 15

24 Dec. 1791 - John PERKINSON and Elizabeth Anderson. Chesterfield Co. C. p. 13

23

10 Mar. 1792 - John PERKINSON and Lyncia Andrews. Chesterfield Co. C.f.14

13 Mar. 1833 - John PERKINSON and Emeline T. Eppes. Prince George Co. M.B.

1 Nov. 1796 - John PATERSON and Susanna Irby Epes. Nottoway Co. C. p.17

8 Jan. 1822 - John A. PETERSON and Virginia Thweatt (Spinster). Prince George Co. M.B.

2 Apr. 1819 - Kennon PERKINSON and Martha Wilkins (wid.). Prince George Co. M.B.

6 Dec. 1788 - William PERRY and Pheby Walthall. Chesterfield Co. C. p.9

2 Mar. 1805 - John PETTUS and Martha Ragsdale. Lunenburg Co. C. p. 18

14 Nov. 1809 - Stephen PETTUS and Susanna Jordan. Lunenburg Co. C. p.19

6 Dec. 1814 - William G. PETTUS and Jane C. Lamkin. Lunenburg Co. C.p.20

26 Feb. 1849 - William J. PINCHBECK and Antoinette Abernathy, at Res. of Mr. Butterworth. B. p. 310

14 Aug. 1788 - John POLLARD and Frances Swanson. Prince George Co. C. p. 9

31 May 1849 - John W. P. POOL and Susanna Moody. Married by Rev. I. E. Hargrave. Dinwiddie Co. Deed Book 6, p. 191

20 Mar. 1888 - David W. POOLE and Ella Tally, at Res. of Mr. J. W. Tally, Dinwiddie Co. B. p. 336

14 Oct. 1786 - John POTTS and Elizabeth Gee. Prince George Co. C.p.4

13 Oct. 1789 - Hardeman POYTHRESS and Elizabeth Golder. Prince George Co. C. p. 10

31 Oct. 1829 - John POYTHRESS and Ann Hollingsworth. Prince George Co. M.B.

10 Feb. 1787 - William POYTHRESS and Elizabeth Blair Bland. Prince George Co. C. p. 6

12 Oct. 1869 - Albert Theodore POWELL and Louisa J. Thweatt, at Res. of Archibald Thweatt of Dinwiddie Co. B. p. 332

5 Mar. 1789 - William PRENTIS and Mary Geddy. Petersburg. C. p. 10

2 Feb. 1863 - Joshua PRETLOW and Ann Elizabeth Butler, at Calvary Church Dinwiddie Co. B. p. 331

1 Oct. 1831 - Christopher PROCTOR and Margaret Rudder. Prince George Co. M.B.

25 Dec. 1847 - Samuel PRYOR and Mrs. Ann E. Broadnax at Kingston, Dinwiddie Co. B. p. 310

7 Oct. 1802 - William PULLY, Jr. and Patsy Thompson. Lunenburg Co. C. p. 18

26 Dec. 1789 - William RAGSDALE and Ann Green Tucker. Prince George Co. C. p. 11

6 Apr. 1786 - William RAMSDEN and Mary Roberts. Petersburg. C. p.4

14 June 1788 - John REABY and Mary Avery. Prince George Co. C. p. 8

16 June 1791 - Jacob REESE and Dyancy Meacham. Sussex Co. C. p. 13

12 Jan. 1838 - Richard E. RICHARDSON and Sally S. Williams. Prince George Co. M.B.

16 Jan. 1833 - Christopher RISPESS and Agness Stackhouse. Prince George Co. M.B.

23 Dec. 1789 - Briggs RIVES and Ann Cureton. Prince George Co. C. p. 11

23 May 1839 - Briggs RIVES (Dr.) and Eliza A.H.B. Wells. Prince George Co. M.B.

16 Dec. 1840 - Edward RIVES and Elizabeth Livesay. Prince George Co. M.B

14 June 1827 - Green RIVES and Susan Woodward at Balaam Wells', Dinwiddie Co. B. p. 300

3 Feb. 1829 - Richard RIVES and Harriet E. Rives, at Thomas Rives', Dinwiddie Co. B. p. 301

28 Jan. 1835 - Robert C. RIVES and Ann Eliza King, at Mr. Miles M. King's Dinwiddie Co. B. p. 305

15 Apr. 1788 - William RIVES and Elizabeth Baugh. Prince George Co. C.p.8

11 Apr. 1818 - William RIVES and Nancy Hackney (Spinster). Prince George Co.

27 Nov. 1830 - William RIVES and Dionysia R. Wells, at Mrs. Wells', Dinwiddie Co. B. p. 302

12 Feb. 1836 - William W. RIVES and Ann Fisher. Prince George Co. M.B.

15 Sept. 1820 - Jesse RIX and Mary Dangerfield (Spinster) Prince George Co. M.B.

2 Jan. 1788 - Francis ROBERTS and Liddy Richardson. Prince George Co. C. p. 8

5 Jan. 1820 - John W. ROBERTS and Mary H. Stackhouse (Spinster). Prince George Co. M.B.

26 Oct. 1797 - Daniel ROBERTSON and Betsy Edmundson. Lunenburg Co. C.p.17

11 June 1799 - Francis ROBERTSON and Mary Jones. Lunenburg Co. C. p.16

16 June 1798 - John ROBERTSON and Polly Davis. Lunenburg Co. C. p. 16

19 Nov. 1795 - John Archer ROBERTSON and Elizabeth Royall. Nottoway Co. C. p. 17

3 _____ 1801 - Warning Peter ROBERTSON and Lucy Mackie. Lunenburg Co. C. p. 16

2 Jan. 1787 -William ROBERTSON and Margaret Duran. Petersburg. C.p.5

20 Dec. 1795 - William ROBERTSON and Elizabeth Jane Mason. Lunenburg Co. C. p. 17

30 Dec. 1797 - William H. ROBERTSON and Susannah Winn. Nottoway Co. C. p. 17

16 June 1825 - William B. ROBINSON and Caroline Williams. Prince George Co. M.B.

9 Dec. 1787 - Jacob ROLLINGS and Mary Riley. Petersburg. C. p. 7

18 July 1822 - Randolph ROPER, Jr. and Martha Ann Eppes (Spinster). Prince George Co. M.B.

23 Dec. 1786 - Burwell ROSSER and Ann Hobbs. Prince George Co. C. p. 5

7 Apr. 1792 - William ROSSER and Susannah Rives. Prince George Co. C.p.14

23 Apr. 1791 - John ROWLETT and Locky Brown. Chesterfield Co. C. p. 12

29 Jan. 1789 - John ROWLETT and Mary Dance. Chesterfield Co. C. p. 10

7 Feb. 1789 - William ROYAL and Sarah Singleton. Prince George Co. C.p.10

24 Nov. 1831 - Thomas RUFFIN and Louisa G. Gilliam, at Mrs. Gilliam's, Brunswick Co. B. p. 302

27 July 1793 - Burwell SADLER and Mary Sturdivant. Prince George Co. C. p. 15

18 July 1826 - James SADLER and Rebecca Stainback. Prince George Co. M.B.

9 May 1831 - Acrill SAVEDGE and Mary S. Hatch. Prince George Co. M.B.

22 Dec. 1830 - John SCARBROUGH and Nancy Anthony. Prince George Co. M.B.

27 Nov. 1788 - William SCOGGIN and Celia Cotton. Sussex Co. C. p. 9

13 June 1791 - Gerreld SCOTT and Amey Dyer. Dinwiddie Co. C. p. 13

25 Mar. 1786 - James SCOT and Nellie Norton. Dinwiddie Co. C. p. 3

3 Sept. 1834 - Peter Edward SCOTT and Harriett Meade, at the Grove, Brunswick Co. B. p. 304

13 Jan. 1829 - Thomas SCOTT and Mary B. Blackwell. Prince George Co. M.B

12 Dec. 1787 - Carter SEWARD and Rebecca Rives. Prince George Co. C. p.7

31 Mar. 1821 - William SHANKS and Frances Williams (Spinster). Prince George Co. M.B.

20 Aug. 1791 - William SHARP and Winefred Timberlake. Dinwiddie Co. C. p. 13

19 Feb. 1838 - Baker A. SHEFFIELD and Mary R. Rives. Prince George Co.M.

19 June 1788 - Patrick M. SHIFFERY and Patsy Johnson. Surry Co. C. p.8

13 Oct. 1785 - John SHORE and Anne Bolling. Petersburg. C. p. 2

14 Dec. 1829 - Ephraim SIMMONS and Sarah H. Price. (Issued in Surry Co.) Prince George Co. M.B.

15 Nov. 1825 - Thomas SIMMONS and Catharine Baird. Prince George Co. M.B

15 June 1786 - William SKINNER and Jenny Black. Petersburg. C. p. 4

2 June 1791 - Lodowick SLATER and Polly James. Petersburg. C. p. 12

24 Mar. 1786 - Christopher SLOKAM and Sally Ash. Petersburg. C. p. 3

8 Nov. 1848 - Albert T. SMITH and Martha P. Lee. Married by I. E. Hargrave. Dinwiddie Co. Deed Book 6, p. 191

10 Dec. 1785 - Archibald SMITH and Lucretia Rosser. Prince George Co. C. p. 3

3 Apr. 1787 - Benjamin SMITH and Ann Buckmire. Petersburg. C. p. 6

24 Feb. 1787 - Clark SMITH and Ann Campbell. Petersburg. C. p. 6

16 May 1803 - James SMITH and Ann Park Street. Lunenburg Co. C. p. 18

10 Nov.1787 - Jesse SMITH and Martha Keys. Chesterfield Co. C. p. 7

16 Sept. 1790 - John SMITH and Sally Dyson. Chesterfield Co. C. p. 11

21 Sept. 1791 - John SMITH and Jane Walch. Petersburg. C. p. 13

9 July 1791 - William SMITH and Mary Adler. Petersburg. C. p. 13

30 Oct. 1833 - Dr. William B. SMITH and Mildred M. Bolling, at Dr. John Feild's, Brunswick Co. B. p. 304

4 May 1807 - John SOMERVELL and Betsy Ann DeGraffenreid. Lunenburg Co. C. p. 19

3 Sept. 1846 - Thomas G. SPILMAN, Esq. and Sarah Jane Freyer, at the Res. of Mrs. Elizabeth Freyer in the City of Baltimore. B. p. 309

27 Nov. 1794 - Melcijah SPRAGINS and Rebecca B. Bolling. Nottoway Co. C. p. 17

3 Nov. 1828 - Peyton STAINBACK and Joanna B. Williams. Prince George M.B.

12 June 1822 - Henry STAUNTON and Eleanor Finney. Prince George Co. M.B.

22 Dec. 1826 - Augustine STEVENS and Mary Hall. Prince George Co. M.B.

17 July 1796 - John STEVENSON and Mary B. Craig. Lunenburg Co. C. p.17

3 May 1792 - Robert STEWART and Amey Goodwyn Raines. Dinwiddie Co. C. p. 14

13 Feb. 1788 - Jesse STILES and Sarah Potter. Chesterfield Co. C.p.8

24 May 1814 - John STOKES and Susanna R. Jones. Lunenburg Co. C.p.20

14 Aug. 1809 - William STOKES and Martha A. Lowry. Lunenburg Co. C.p.19

18 July 1793 - Edmund STONE and Sarah Baugh. Petersburg. C. p. 15

12 May 1792 - Lancelot STONE and Elizabeth Baugh. Petersburg. C.p. 14

7 Apr. 1830 - Dr. Alexander G. STRACHAM and Mary G. Boisseau, at Mrs. Cogbill's, Dinwiddie Co. B. p. 302

16 Oct. 1798 - David STREET and Sarah Stokes. Lunenburg Co. C. p. 16

24 Nov. 1798 - Waddy STREET and Elizabeth Smith. Lunenburg Co. C.p. 16

25 July 1789 - Robert STUART, Jr. and Sally Haldane. Petersburg. C.p.10

22 Jan. 1788 - James STURDIVANT and Patsey Burchett. Prince George Co. C. p. 8

6 Dec. 1832 - Joel STURDIVANT and Sarah Frances Proctor. Prince George Co. M.B.

28 Jan. 1790 - John STURDIVANT and Lucretia Sadler. Prince George Co. C. p. 11

4 Feb. 1830 - Joseph STURDIVANT and Mary Elliott, at Mr. Abner Adam's B. p. 302

26 Sept. 1822 - William STURDIVANT and Elizabeth F. Mann. Prince George Co. M.B.

7 May 1792 - Simon SWAIL and Martha Browder. Petersburg. C. p. 14

12 May 1791 - George SWINBROD and Patsey Barrow. Prince George Co. C. p. 12

27 Sept. 1806 - Rev. Andrew SYME and Jean Cameron. Lunenburg Co. C.p.19

14 July 1791 - Bartley TACKETT and Sarah Wren. Prince George Co. C.p.13

5 Dec. 1825 - Charles H. TATUM and Nancy Williams. Prince George Co. M.B.

18 Jan. 1827 - Epes TATUM and Huldah Williams. Prince George Co. M.B.

16 Oct. 1835 - Eppes TATUM and Adaline J. Gill. Prince George Co. M.B.

15 Feb. 1837 - Robert W. S. TATUM and Martha B. Harris. Prince George Co. M.B.

1 Mar. 1792 - Eppes TEMPLE and Elizabeth Peebles. Prince George Co. C.p.14

14 Feb. 1809 - Edmund F. TAYLOR and Petronilla Lamkin. Lunenburg Co. C. p. 19

15 Nov. 1803 - John TAYLOR and Elizabeth Jones. Lunenburg Co. C. p. 18

28 Oct. 1800 - Thomas TAYLOR and Martha C. Hamblin. Mecklenburg Co. C. p. 16

11 Feb. 1792 - Joshua TEMPLE and Martha Williams. Prince George Co. C. p. 14

1 June 1786 - James TENCH and Sarah Williams. Prince George Co. C. p. 4

17 May 1788 - Thomas TENNEY and Elizabeth Temple. Prince George Co. C.p.8

15 Nov. 1792 - Benjamin THOMAS and Elizabeth Young. Petersburg. C. p. 14

24 Dec. 1785 - James THOMPSON and Sarah Newall. Prince George Co. C. p.3

14 Mar. 1837 - James A. THOMPSON and Mary M. Hobbs. Prince George Co. M.B

18 May 1786 - Francis THOMPSON and Rebeckah Harvie. Petersburg. C. p. 4

10 Sept. 1788 - William THOMPSON and Lucy Herbert Cocke. Sussex Co. C. p. 9

22 Dec. 1836 - William H. THOMPSON and Rebecca A. Hobbs. Prince George Co. M.B.

17 Jan. 1787 - William THOMPSON and Frances Rives. Prince George Co. C. p. 5

8 Dec. 1792 - William THOMSON and Nancy Blakely. Petersburg. C.p.14

19 Jan. 1830 - James W. THWEATT and Elizabeth N. Rives, at Charles Williamson's. B. p. 302

28 July 1787 - Peter THWEATT and Lucretia Parish. Dinwiddie Co. C.p.6

3 Oct. 1834 - Henry TINCH and Elizabeth Williams. Prince George M.B.

15 Feb. 1839 - James TINNEY and Wilmouth A. Wamack. Prince George Co. M.B.

11 Feb. 1786 - William TIMBERLAKE and Elizabeth Turnbull. Petersburg C. p. 3

15 June 1793 - Richard TITMARSH and Sarah Baxter. Prince George Co. C. p. 15

11 Nov. 1829 - Wyatt TITMARSH and Sarah B. Williams. Prince George Co. M.B.

2 Aug. 1837 - Josiah TITMASH and Susan E. Temple. Prince George M.B.

12 Mar. 1791 - James TODD and Frances Cotton. Prince George Co. C. p. 12

26 Mar. 1788 - Benjamin TOTTY and Mary Blankinship. Chesterfield Co. C. p. 8

10 Jan. 1793 - Robert TOTTY and Sandal Andrews. Chesterfield Co. C. p. 15

16 Jan. 1800 - Joseph TOWNES and Susanna Cralle. Lunenburg Co. C. p. 16

12 Jan. 1789 - Buckner TRAYLOR and Mary Handy. Chesterfield Co. C. p. 10

1 Oct. 1801 - Thomas TREDWAY and Jean Lockhead. Lunenburg Co. C. p. 16 and Cumberland Par. p.316

10 Apr. 1828 - Robert TRIPLETT and Virginia Ann Pegram, at Gen. Pegram's, Dinwiddie Co. B. p. 300

Feb. court 1789 - David TUCKER and Frances Jackson. Dinwiddie Co. Order Book 1789-1791, p. 4 (Marriage Contract)

13 Feb. 1787 — Robert TUCKER and Sarah Parham.' Prince George Co. C. p. 6

26 June 1833 — Dr. Sterling H. TUCKER and Martha R. Feild, at Dr. John Feild's, Brunswick Co.   B. p. 303

14 Nov. 1876 — William C. TUCKER of Brunswick Co. and Helen L. Scott of Dinwiddie Co., at Res. of Dr. John L. Scott, father of bride. B. p. 332

19 Dec. 1820 — Richard TUDOR and Susanna J. Stainback (Spinster). Prince George Co. M.B.

20 Aug. 1786 — Hugh TULLOCH and Elizabeth Thomas. Petersburg. C. p. 4

21 June 1837 — Charles TURNBULL and Sarah E. Lashley, at Mrs. Riddick's, Lawrenceville.   B. p. 306

17 Dec. 1829 — Dr. Robert H. TURNBULL and Martha J. Crichton, at Mrs. James Crichton's, Brunswick Co. B. p. 301

14 June 1786 — George TURNER and Lurany Russell. Petersburg. C. p. 4

24 Feb. 1798 — Matthew TURNER and Mary Ingram. Lunenburg Co. C. p. 16

29 Apr. 1818 — John TYRE and Martha Avery (widow). Prince George Co. M.B.

7 Oct. 1786 — William UNDERHILL and Mary Ann Caroline Meachum. Sussex Co. C. p. 4

8 May 1849 — John W. VADEN and Harriet P. Wells. Married by Rev. I. E. Hargrave. Dinwiddie Co. Deed Book 6, p. 191

24 Dec. 1791 — Joseph VADEN and Sarah Ford. Dinwiddie Co. C. p. 13

11 July 1793 — Lemuel VADEN and Winny Blankenship. Chesterfield Co. C. p. 15

11 Dec. 1785 — James VALENTINE and Anne Owens. Petersburg. C. p. 3

17 Apr. 1785 — Ephraim VAUGHAN and Parthena Ridout. Dinwiddie Co. C.p.2

1 Nov. 1809 — John VAUGHAN and Sally Thompson. Lunenburg Co. C. p. 19

28 Aug. 1874 — Peter VAUGHAN and Elizabeth Raines. Prince George Co. C. p. 1

18 Oct. 1786 — Peter VAUGHAN and Mary Godwyn Boisseau. Dinwiddie Co. C. p. 5

15 Jan. 1788 — David VENTRIS and Jenny Dixon. Prince George Co. C. p. 8

1 Mar. 1786 — Noel WADDILL and Eliza L.' Watkins. Petersburg. C. p. 3

14 Sept. 1824 — Edward WALKER and Rebecca Moody. Prince George Co. M.B.

11 Feb. 1830 – John A. WALKER and Authea M. L. Cargill, at Col. John Cargill's, Sussex Co. B. p. 302

27 Mar. 1824 – Isham WAMACK and Critty Patton (widow). Prince George Co. M.B.

18 Feb. 1835 – Travis H. WAMACK and Rozena Wamack. Prince George Co. M.B.

17 Mar. 1785 – Joseph WATKINS and Polly Bushell. Dinwiddie Co. C. p. 2

7 Mar. 1788 – Joseph WEISIGER and Anna Baird. Prince George Co. C. p. 8

19 July 1787 – Thomas WELCH and Jane Edgar. Prince George Co. C. p. 6

3 Apr. 1790 – David WELLS and Eliza Wamock. Petersburg. C. p. 11

20 Dec. 1832 – Green J. WELLS and Mrs. Martha G. Hawkins, at Philomon Hawkins', Dinwiddie Co. B. p. 303

25 Feb. 1886 – John D. T. WELLS and Mary A. Clark, at Res. of Mr.Andrew Clark, Dinwiddie Co. B. p. 335

16 Jan. 1849 – William B. WELLS and Mary E. Sturdivant. Married by Rev. I. E. Hargrave. Dinwiddie Co. Deed Book 6, p. 191

4 Nov. 1790 – John WEST and Elizabeth Mitchell Jones. Prince George Co. C. p. 12

9 July 1786 – Joseph WESTMORE and Elizabeth Baird. Prince George Co. C. p. 4

2 Nov. 1831 – James WHITE and Sarah Marks. Prince George Co. M.B.

30 Oct. 1800 – William WHITE and Polly Vaden Jackson. Lunenburg Co. C. p. 16

30 Nov. 1790 – William WHITEHEAD and Clarissa Lamb. Petersburg. C. p.12

9 Nov. 1832 – Charles H. WHITMORE and Lucy Ann Rives, at Mrs. Rives', Dinwiddie Co. B. p. 303

28 Jan. 1828 – David WHITMORE and Elizabeth Ann Johnson. Prince George Co. M. B.

30 Jan. 1794 – Thomas WILKES and Sally Gunn. Nottoway Co. C. p. 17

23 Dec. 1822 – Edmund WILKINS and Elizabeth D. Gary (Spinster). Prince George Co. M. B.

5 Apr. 1827 – John L. WILKINS, Jr. and Ann Brodnax, at William E. Brodnax's, Brunswick Co. B. p. 300

16 Oct. 1820 – William C. WILKINS and Elizabeth Wilkins (Spinster). Prince George Co. M.B.

23 July 1829 – Dr. William Webb WILKINS and Mary A. Beasley, at Dr. Beasley's, Brunswick Co.   B. p. 301

12 Aug. 1789 – Frederick WILKINSON and Patsey McDowell. Prince George Co.   C. p. 10

9 Oct. 1806 – David G. WILLIAMS and Mary E. P. Doswell. Nottoway Co. C. p. 19

15 Dec. 1787 – David WILLIAMS and Mary Peebles. Sussex Co. C. p. 7

15 Aug. 1823 – Grief WILLIAMS and Mary Ann Newcomb (widow). Prince George Co. M.B.

25 Aug. 1785 – James WILLIAMS and Patsey Fewqua. Prince George Co. C.p.

4 Feb. 1835 – James WILLIAMS and Sally Anne Smith. Prince George Co. M.B

21 Dec. 1809 – Joseph G. WILLIAMS and Catharine Fitzgerald. Nottoway Co. C. p. 19

20 Dec. 1848 – Leroy A. WILLIAMS and Lucy T. Moody. Married by Rev. I.E. Hargrave. Dinwiddie Co. Deed Book 6, p. 191

23 Dec. 1830 – Richard WILLIAMS and Harriet Williams. Prince George Co.M

30 Apr. 1829 – Rodrick WILLIAMS and Elizabeth Williams. Prince George Co

9 July 1807 – Samuel G. WILLIAMS and Gracie B. Cowan. Lunenburg Co. C.p.

24 Apr. 1838 – Uriah WILLIAMS and Susan Tench. Prince George Co. M.B.

10 Sept. 1789 – William WILLIAMS and Betty Anderson. Prince George Co. C. p. 10

5 Jan. 1788 – William WILLIAMS and Martha Reese. Prince George Co. C. p.8

23 Oct. 1818 – William WILLIAMS and Martha Sheffield (Spinster). Prince George Co. M.B.

20 Dec. 1855 – Richard W. WILLIAMSON and Josephine Sturdivant, at Mr.Bette B. p. 311

13 Apr. 1824 – William WILLIAMS and Susan Stainback (window). Prince Georg Co. M. B.

13 Jan. 1785 – William WILLS and Mary Watkins. Dinwiddie Co. C. p. 2

19 Mar. 1789 – George WILSON and Mary Ann Banister. Petersburg. C. p. 10

17 Oct. 1789 – George WILSON and Dinny Browder.   Prince George Co. C.p.1

24 Dec. 1829 – Legrand W. WILSON and Catharine M. Bourdon, at Mrs. Mary Bolling's.   B. p. 302

18 Oct. 1788 - Abraham WOMACK and Joanna Livesay. Prince George Co.
C. p. 8

14 Mar. 1823 - Frederick WOMACK and Joanna Nancy Livesay (Spinster).
Prince George Co. M.B.

9 Aug. 1828 - Jesse WOMACK and Martha Ann Jamison. Prince George Co.M.B.

9 June 1791 - William WOMACK and Elizabeth Perkinson. Chesterfield
Co. C. p. 12

14 Dec. 1793 - Francis WOOLFOLK and Eliza Taylor. Sussex Co. C.p.15

22 Dec. 1785 - Jesse WRENIE and Mary Hall. Sussex Co. C.p.3

6 Feb. 1884 - John J. WYATT and Helen Heartwell, at Res. of
H.J. Heartwell. B. p. 334

9 Oct. 1828 - Benjamin F. WYCHE and Margaret B. Cargill, at John
Cargill's. Sussex Co. B. p. 301

24 July 1788 - Benjamin WYCHE and Elizabeth Mason. Sussex Co.
C. p. 9

9 Dec. 1784 - Joshua WYNNE and Mary Todd. Dinwiddie Co. C.p.1

7 July 1784 - Duncan YOUNG and Susannah Womack. Dinwiddie Co. C.p.1

21 Aug. 1787 - Duncan YOUNG and Mary Moore. Petersburg. C.p.6

25 Dec. 1786 - Henry YOUNG and Winney Tucker Goodwyn. Dinwiddie Co.
C.p.5

16 June 1825 - James A. YOUNG and Eleanor F. Birchett. Prince George
Co. M.B.

20 Jan. 1788 - William YOUNG and Eleanor Healy. Petersburg. C.p.8

26 June 1850 - Charles G. ZEHMER (Dr.) and Jane Manlove Bourdon,
at Res. of Mr. Bourdon. B. p. 310

A

Abernathy,
    Antoinette   23
    Catherine   18
    M. E.   20

Adler,
    Mary   27

Allen,
    Jane (See Harrison)   10

Alley,
    Winefred   8

Anderson,
    Betty   32
    Elizabeth   2, 22
    Mary   5

Andrews,
    Elizabeth   19
    Frances   22
    Lyncia   23
    Polly   21
    Sandal   29

Andross,
    Anne   12

Anthony,
    Nancy   25

Armistead,
    Euphan   11

Ash,
    Sally   26

Aspey,
    Mary   22

Avery,
    Martha   30
    Mary   24

B

Bacon,
    Mary A. G.   22
    Sally G.   17

Bacon,
    Susanna R.   3

Backus,
    Julia Ann   11

Bagley,
    Mary Chappel   21

Baird,
    Anna   31
    Catharine   26
    Elizabeth   31

Banister,
    Mary Ann   32

Barlow,
    Elizabeth   7

Barrow,
    Patsey   28

Batte,
    Mary   13

Baugh,
    Elizabeth   24, 27
    Sarah   27

Baxter,
    Sarah   29

Beasley,
    Mary A.   32

Beeglesien,
    Elizabeth Susan   4

Berry,
    Martha   6

Billups,
    Jane F.   5

Birchett,
    Eleanor F.   33

Birckett,
    Elizabeth   10

Black,
    Jenny   26

Blackwell,
    Martha A. E.   10
    Mary B.   26

Blakely,
    Mary   7
    Nancy   29

Bland,
    Elizabeth Blair   23

Blankenship,
    Winny   30

Blankinship,
    Mary   29

Boisseau,
    Mary G.   27
    Mary Godwyn   30

Bolling,
    Anne   26
    Frances   18
    Lucy Ann   7
    Martha Emily   16
    Mary H.   10
    Mildred M.   27
    Rebecca B.   27

Bonner,
    Mary   11
    Mary Heath   3
    Polly   18

Booker,
    Elizabeth   14

Bourdon,
    Catharine M.   32
    Jane Manlove   33

Bowers,
    Betsy   3

Boyd,
    Jane A.   14
    Nancy   14

Bradley,
    Ann   19

Brockwell,
    Ann   16

Brodnax,
    Ann   31
    Ann E. (Mrs.)   24
    Anne   5
    Mary Louisa   2

Browder,
    Dinny   32
    Martha   28

Brown,
    Elizabeth Adeline   6
    Frances Lowry   12
    Locky   25
    Lucy   11
    Mary   12

Buckmire,
    Ann   26

Buford,
    Catharine   5

Buford,
    Frances   5

Bugg,
    Anne   18

Burchett,
    Patsey   27

Burrow,
    Mariah P.   15

Burton,
    Anne   13

Burwell,
    Frances Powell   17
    Matilda   3
    Panthea   3

Bushell,
    Polly   31

Butler,
    Ann Elizabeth   23
    Martha   6

Butterworth,
    Rebecca   11

C

Cain,
- Betty — 22
- Mason — 14
- Susanna — 12

Caleb,
- Charlotte — 17

Cameron,
- Jean — 28
- Mary Read — 1

Campbell,
- Ann — 26
- Frances H. — 9

Cargill,
- Authea M. L. — 31
- Lucy B. — 22
- Margaret B. — 33
- Sarah H. — 20

Cate,
- Milly — 20

Chambers,
- Anne W. — 7
- Martha C. — 2
- Sally — 7

Chambliss,
- Betsey — 13

Chapel,
- Elizabeth — 15

Chappell,
- Eliza — 13
- Martha — 21

Clark,
- Elizabeth — 15
- Mary A. — 31

Clarke,
- Mahala — 9

Clements,
- Margaret — 13
- Susannah — 4

Cleveland,
- Martha — 2

Cocke,
- Ann J. — 9
- Lucy Herbert — 28
- Mary — 16

Cogbill,
- Frances — 1

Colvin (alias)
- See Jesse Caldwell — 5

Comer,
- Mary W. — 20
- Pamela A. — 17

Conaway,
- Sally C. — 20

Cook,
- Polly — 2
- Sarah — 20

Cosby,
- Melinda — 7

Cotton,
- Celia — 26
- Frances — 29

Covington,
- Elizabeth — 6

Cowan,
- Gracie B. — 32

Craig,
- Frances — 13
- Mary B. — 27

Cralle,
- Susanna — 29

Crenshaw,
- Jane — 5

Crichton,
- Martha J. — 30

Cross,
- Rebecca — 9

Crowder,
- Elizabeth — 18

Crump,
- Maria Ann — 1

Cummings,
- Sally W. — 13

Cunningham,
   Obedience   19

Cureton,
   Ann   24

Cutler,
   Susan G.   20

D

Dance,
   Mary   25
   Rhode   16

Dangerfield,
   Mary   24

Daniel,
   Lucy   18
   Maria Frances   18
   Patsey   2

Davenport,
   Nancy   8
   Susannah   17

Davis,
   Elizabeth D.   16
   Polly   25

Deahart,
   Lucretia   8

DeGraffenreid,
   Betsy-Ann   27

Dixon,
   Jenny   30

Dodd,
   Margaret   9

Donaldson,
   Ann   9

Donnell,
   Eleanor M.   18

Doswell,
   Mary E. P.   32

Downing,
   Christianna   7

Downman,
   Elizabeth Osborne   15

Draper,
   Nancy   11

Dunn,
   Ann   2
   Elizabeth   15

Duran,
   Margaret   25
   Mary   19

Dyer,
   Amey   26

Dyson,
   Sally   26

E

Eckles,
   Sally   16

Edgar,
   Jane   31

Edmunds,
   Mary   18

Edmundson,
   Betsy   25

Edwards,
   Elizabeth   5
   Susannah   19

Eldridge,
   Mary   3
   Paulina B.   9

Elliott,
   Mary   28

Ellis,
   Mary   17

Emery,
   Elizabeth   21

Epes,
   Catharine G.   7
   Effee   22

Epes,
  Martha   16
  Susanna Irby   23

Eppes,
  Christian   12
  Eliza   15
  Elizabeth   19
  Elizabeth Taylor   8
  Emeline T.   23
  Martha Ann   25
  Mary   1

Epps,
  Catharine W.   13

Erskine,
  Martha   17

Evans,
  Pricilla   2
  Martha   13

F

Falkner,
  Margaret   4

Fallett,
  Catherine   17

Feild,
  Martha R.   30
  Susan E.   17

Fewqua,
  Mary S.   19
  Patsey   32

Field,
  Nellie   18
  Mary   12

Finn,
  Amey   21

Finney,
  Eleanor   27

Fisher,
  Ann   21, 24

Fitzgerald,
  Catharine   32
  Elizabeth   16

Flack,
  Mildred   19

Folkes,
  Elizabeth H.   12
  Mary Ann   8
  Nancy   21

Ford,
  Sarah   30

Freeman,
  Kesiah   21

Freyer,
  Sarah Jane   27

Friend,
  Mary   7

G

Garland,
  Frances   8

Gary,
  Elizabeth D.   31
  Mary E.   6
  Pamela   11
  Sarah N.   9

Geddy,
  Mary   23

Gee,
  Elizabeth   23

Gibbs,
  Dorothy V.   2

Gill,
  Adaline J.   28
  Anna   6
  Jency   11
  Jinny   9
  Lucy H.   22
  Mary   11
  Rebecca T.   12

Gilliam,
  Anne   8
  Elizabeth   5
  Louisa G.   25
  Roberta C. P.   4
  Susan J.   10

Glassco,			Haldane,	
Fanny	12		Sally	27
Glover,			Hall,	
Elizabeth	1		Mary	27, 33
			Rebecca	5
Golder,				
Elizabeth	23		Halsey,	
			Elizabeth K.	17
Goodwyn,				
Paulona	22		Hamblin,	
Winney Tucker	33		Martha C.	28
Gracie,			Hamilton,	
Mary	21		Isabella	19
Grammer,			Hammond,	
Frankey	18		Judy	21
Lucy	17			
Mary	2		Handy,	
			Mary	29
Granger,				
Elizabeth	12		Hardaway,	
Margaret	13		Lucy	13
			Mason	8
Grantham,			Susan A.	14
Parthena J.A.E.	13			
			Hare,	
Green,			Mary Ann	6
Lucy	9			
Lucy B.	20		Harmon,	
			Ann N.	4
Griffin,				
Mary	1		Harris,	
			Frances E.	4
Gunn,			Martha B.	28
Sally	31			
			Harrison,	
H			Alice	16
			Ann Carter	6
Hacker,			Eliza	1
Obedience	8		Elizabeth	4
			Jane (See Allen)	10
Hackney,			Jane Pleasant	22
Alivia Ann	15		Mary	22
Ann	10		Nancy	7
Frances	21		Virgilla A.	5
Nancy	24			
Sarah	13		Harvie,	
			Rebeckah	28
Hair,				
Mary	1			

Haskins,		Holden,	
Susan E.	20	Elizabeth	17
Hatch,		Hollingsworth,	
Mary S.	25	Ann	23
Hattaway,		Holloway,	
Elizabeth	5	Sarah	6
Hawkins,		Holmes,	
Martha G. (Mrs.)	31	Margaret B.	4
Sarah	10		
Susie T.	6	Holsey,	
		Millender	7
Hawthorne,			
Betsey	14	Holt,	
		Fanny	14
Healy,			
Eleanor	33	Hopkins,	
		Frances	17
Heartwell,			
Helen	33	Hoy,	
Roberta	16	Anne	11
Heath,		Hunnicutt,	
Cynthia	1	Mary	3
Milly	11	Rachel	16

I

Heth,			
Nancy	14	Inglish,	
		Priscilla	7
Hite,			
Henrietta A.	5	Ingram,	
Jane	8	Mary	30
Mary	15		
		Irby,	
Hobbs,		Tobitha	4
Ann	25		
Jemima	2	Irvin,	
Mary M.	28	Courtney	14
Mildred	7		
Rebecca A.	29		

J

Hodge,			
Sarah	9	Jackson,	
		Frances	29
Hodges,		Polly Vaden	31
Elizabeth	7		
		James,	
Hogan,		Polly	26
Margaret	6		
		Jamison,	
Holcombe,		Martha Ann	33
Virginia E.	2		

Jeffries,
Salley   1

Johnson,
A. E.   11
Elizabeth Ann   31
Patsy   26

Jolly,
Mary Ann   20

Jones,
Ann Elizabeth   16
Elizabeth   17, 28
Elizabeth Mitchell   31
Frances   10
Lucy B.   20
Martha   6
Mary   20, 25
Rebecca   2
Rebeccah Edwards   17
Sally   7, 19
Sarah   7, 15
Susanna R.   27

Jordan,
Susanna   23

K

Kerr,
Elizabeth   21

Keys,
Martha   26

King,
Anne   11
Ann Eliza   24

L

Lamb,
Clarissa   31

Lamkin,
Jane C.   23
Mary Epes Jones   14
Petronilla   28

Lanier,
Lucy   21
Martha   19

Lanthrope,
Patsey C.   12

Lany,
Elizabeth   11

Lashley,
Sarah E.   30

Leath,
Jemimah   21

Ledbetter,
Lucy Ann   11
Martha E.   3

Lee,
Agness   17
Celia   7
Lucy   1
Martha P.   26

Lesenbery,
Lucy   18

Lessenberry,
Sally   3

Lewis,
Elizabeth   20
Martha (Mrs.)   6
Sylvia   4

Livesay,
Catharine H.   4
Eliza   14
Elizabeth   24
Harriet   19
Joanna   33
Joanna Nancy   33
Lucretia   17
Mary   4, 15
Milly   18
Patsy   4
Rebecca   20
Sally   18

Lockhead,
Eliza   12
Jean   29

Lone,
Mary   2

Long,		Marks,	
Mary	2	Mary R.	9
		Polly	19
Lowry,		Sarah	31
Martha A.	27		
		Mason,	
Lubbock,		Elizabeth	33
Jane R.	4	Elizabeth Jane	25

Mc

		Massenburg,	
MacFarlane,		Elizabeth	22
Margaret	3	Lucy	20
McCullock,		Meacham,	
Anne	6	Dyancy	24
McDowell,		Meachum,	
Lettice	8	Mary Ann Caroline	30
Patsey	32	Winney	6
McLaughlan,		Meade,	
Elizabeth	22	Aurelia	12
		Harriett	26
McLeane,		Marietta E.	3
Betsey	1		
		Meredith,	

M

		Martha D.	5
Macken,		Mitchell,	
Letty	8	Frances	3
		Winifred G.	19
Mackie,			
Lucy	25	Moody,	
		Elizabeth Y.	4
Maclin,		Leah	22
Sarah E.	22	Lucy Ann	20
		Lucy T.	32
Major,		Martha L.	7
Rebeccah	12	Phoebe	9
		Rebecca	30
Manlove,		Sarah B.	21
Ann, (Mrs.)	12	Susanna	23
Mann,		Moor,	
Elizabeth F.	28	Dorothy	2
Mary	22		
		Moore,	
Manson,		Elizabeth	5, 16
Martha	5	Jane	21
		Lucy	3
Marks,		Martha	4
Barbara	7	Mary	14,33
Eliza A.	15		

Moore,
| Nanny | 1 |
| Sarah Chappell | 18 |

Moran,
| Ann | 17 |

Morison,
Ann	14
Jane	13
Patience	9

Murphy
| Mary Ann | 9 |

Murray,
| Mary | 14 |

N

Nash,
| Martha W. | 3 |

Newall,
| Sarah | 28 |

Newbill,
| Virginia H. | 19 |

Newcomb,
| Mary Ann | 32 |

Newell,
| Elizabeth D. | 8 |

Newsum,
| Sarah | 12 |

Nicholson,
| Lucy W. | 7 |
| Mary | 10 |

Norton,
| Betsey | 1 |
| Nellie | 26 |

O

Osborne,
| Anne | 14 |

Owens,
| Anne | 30 |

P

Parham,
| Sarah | 30 |

Parish,
| Lucretia | 29 |

Park,
| Nancy | 21 |

Patrick,
| Sarah | 3 |

Patterson,
| Rebecca | 10 |

Patton,
| Critty | 31 |

Peebles,
Agnes	15
Elizabeth	28
Mary	32
Sarah L.	8
Susannah	11

Pegram,
Maria Ward	20
Matilda C.	4
Virginia Ann	29

Pennington,
| Ursella | 5 |

Perkenson,
| Mason | 1 |

Perkerson,
| Betsey | 5 |

Perkins,
Adelia V.	2
Elizabeth	16
Mary E. A.	22

Perkinson,
Elizabeth	33
Lucy A.	21
Pricilla	22
Susan	15

Peter,
| Clara H. | 7 |

Peterson,
    Alley   16
    Amelia   16

Pettus,
    Harriott   17
    Polly L.   17
    Sally D.   9

Phillips,
    Nancy Thomas   14

Pool
    Julia A. P.   14

Potter,
    Sarah   27

Poythress,
    Agnes   1
    Elizabeth B.   19
    Susanna   3, 19

Price,
    Sarah H.   26
    Susan E. L.   19

Pritchard,
    Martha   16

Proctor,
    Elizabeth   11
    Sarah Frances   27

R

Ragsdale,
    Martha   23

Raines,
    Amey Goodwyn   27
    Becky   13
    Elizabeth   30

Randolph,
    Lucy B.   3
    Maria   13

Redwood,
    Anne   14

Reese,
    Martha   32

Richardson,
    Judith   8
    Liddy   24

Riddlehurst,
    Mary   1

Ridout,
    Parthena   30

Riley,
    Mary   25

Rives,
    Elizabeth Atkins   22
    Elizabeth N.   29
    Frances   29
    Harriet E.   24
    Judith   3, 11, 15
    Lucy Ann   31
    Mary R.   26
    Rebecca   26
    Rebecca C.   15
    Sarah   22
    Susannah   25

Roberts,
    Mary   24

Robertson,
    Mary   2

Roffe,
    Jane A. E.   9

Rosser,
    Lucretia   26

Royall,
    Elizabeth   25
    Winifred   2

Rudder,
    Margaret   23

Russell,
    Frances   12
    Lurany   30
    Rebeckah   21

S

Sadler,	
Lucretia	28
Sandys,	
Milly T.	6
Saunders,	
Patty	7
Scott,	
Helen L.	30
Jean	17
Martha H.	10
Sears,	
Miriam	7
Seegood,	
Mima	5
Shackleford,	
Dicey	11
Sheffield,	
Jane	5
Martha	32
Shepherd,	
Nancy	1
Silvie,	
Mary	12
Simmons,	
Elizabeth Mansell	12
Singleton,	
Sarah	25
Smith,	
Celah	20
Elizabeth	27
Mary	6
Sally Anne	32
Spain,	
Martha A. M.	20
Stackhouse,	
Agness	24
Elizabeth	8
Mary H.	25

Stacy,	
Eliza	1
Stafford,	
Elizabeth	7
Stainback,	
Anne	14
Elizabeth	10
Mary	9
Rebecca	25
Susanna J.	30
Susan	32
Stephens,	
Nancy	2
Stevens,	
Poline	18
Stevenson,	
Martha A.	18
Mary B.	18
Stewart,	
Jane	10
Stith,	
Minerva	16
Stokes,	
Sally M.	2
Sarah	27
Susanna	5
Stout,	
Mary N.	8
Street,	
Ann Park	26
Sturdivant,	
Elizabeth	2
Josephine	32
Mary	4, 25
Mary E.	31
Sarah	6
Swanson,	
Frances	23
Swepson,	
Susanna	8

T

Tally,
Ella 23

Tarry,
Rebecca 20

Tatum,
Amijane 2

Taylor,
Eliza 33

Temple,
Elizabeth 28
Mary A. 17
Nancy 10
Susan E. 29

Tench,
Sukey 16
Susan 32

Thomas,
Elizabeth 30

Thompson,
Mary Shaw 14
Patsy 24
Rebecca 21
Sally 30

Thrift,
Augusta 18
Joannah 8

Thweatt,
Betty 9
Louisa J. 23
Lucy C. 3
Mary H. 3
Susan 10
Virginia 23

Timberlake,
Winefred 26

Titmash,
Pamila 10
Elizabeth 12

Todd,
Anne 4
Mary 33

Totty,
Margaret 8

Traylor,
Susan R. 11

Tucker,
Ann Green 24

Turnbull,
Anne 22
Eliza Jane 20
Elizabeth 29

Tyus,
Pamelia 16

U

Underhill,
Elizabeth 14
Mary 11, 14

V

Vaughan,
Frances 13
Martha 2

W

Walch,
Jane 27

Walker,
Tabitha 3
Mary R. H. 15

Walthall,
Anne 19
Mary 14
Pheby 23

Wamack,
Rozena 31
Wilmouth A. 29

Wamock,
Eliza 31

Ward,
Catharine 10
Prudence 16

Wortham,
    Lucy   1

Wren,
    Sarah   28

Wynn,
    Susan W.   8

<u>Y</u>

Young,
    Ann H.   10
    Elizabeth   28
    Rebeccah   15

www.ingramcontent.com/pod-product-compliance
Lightning Source LLC
Chambersburg PA
CBHW021839020426
42334CB00014B/699